Histoires naturelles

ONEWORLD CLASSICS LTD
London House
243-253 Lower Mortlake Road
Richmond
Surrey TW9 2LL
United Kingdom
www.oneworldclassics.com

Histoires naturelles first published in French in 1909
This translation first published by Oneworld Classics Limited in 2010
Translation and introduction © Richard Stokes, 2010
Illustrations and cover image © Lucinda Rogers, 2010

Printed in Great Britain by CPI Antony Rowe, Chippenham, Wiltshire

ISBN: 978-1-84749-170-1

Jules Renard
Histoires naturelles

Translated by Richard Stokes
Illustrations by Lucinda Rogers

ONEWORLD
CLASSICS

Contents

Introduction

Students of French know *Poil de Carotte*, Renard's autobiographical tales about the sufferings of a sensitive child who is bullied by his mother and neglected by his father; musicians and singers are familiar with five of his poems from *Histoires naturelles*, set to music of genius by Maurice Ravel in 1906; admirers of Julian Barnes's recent memoir, *Nothing to Be Frightened of*, will be aware of Renard's wonderfully epigrammatic *Journal*; and lovers of art may have encountered *Histoires naturelles* through the illustrations of Toulouse-Lautrec and Pierre Bonnard. For the rest, this great writer (Albert Thibaudet called Renard 'un des plus grands écrivains de son temps') is largely unknown in English-speaking countries.

He was born on 22nd February 1864 in Châlons-du-Maine. His father, who worked on the construction of the local railway, moved to Chitry-les-Mines in 1866, where he later became Mayor. From 1875–81, Jules and his older brother attended a boarding-school in Nevers. Despite failing the first part of his *baccalauréat*, Renard was finally accepted at the École Normale Supérieure in Paris, which he left before completing his studies.

Aged twenty-four, he begins to eke out a living as a writer; he frequents the literary cafés, writes poetry that an actress friend, Danièle Davyle, recites in the *salons*. A year's military service follows in Bourges. 1886 sees the publication of a volume of poems, *Les*

Roses, which is reviewed by Camille Delaville in *La Revue verte*. He starts working as a journalist for several newspapers. 'Tout vaut mieux que de retourner à Chitry,' he writes to his father.

He stays in Paris and supplements his meagre allowance by tutoring three children and working as a secretary for their father. In 1888 he marries the seventeen-year-old Marie Morneau. The substantial dowry enables him to publish a volume of short stories, *Crime de village*, dedicated to his father. His first child is born in February 1889. At the end of the year he founds the *Mercure de France* with other young writers, a paper for which he writes regular articles over the next few years. In 1890 Lemerre publishes *Sourires pincés*, a volume containing nine of the tales that will eventually appear in *Poil de Carotte*. He immerses himself in Paris, frequents the theatre, pays regular visits to Alphonse Daudet and establishes contact with writers such as Marcel Schwob and André Gide, who later declares that he reads Renard 'comme un classique'. His first major prose work, *L'Écornifleur*, appears in 1892 to critical acclaim. *Coquecigrues* and *La Lanterne sourde* are published in 1893, *Le Vigneron dans sa vigne* and *Poil de Carotte* in 1894. He makes the acquaintance of several artists, including Steinlen, Vallotton and Toulouse-Lautrec, all of whom will illustrate his work. His fame gradually spreads.

'Le Chasseur d'images', the first piece of the *Histoires naturelles*, is published in 1895 in 'La Nouvelle Revue'. Renard widens his circle of friends and meets Edmond Rostand who introduces him to Sarah Bernhardt. He attends the funeral of Paul Verlaine in 1896, a year which sees the first edition of *Histoires naturelles*, that contains forty-five texts. He rents an old vicarage at Chaumot, near Chitry, and calls it 'La Gloriette', which is also his pet name for Marie, and from now on spends his holidays there – the surrounding countryside will inspire many of the pages of the *Histoires naturelles*. He hires two servants to look after his property in the country: Simon Chalumeau (Philippe from 'La mort de Brunette' and 'Le lièvre' in *Histoires naturelles*, the factotum who features in much of Renard's work, correspondence and the *Journal*); and his wife – the 'Ragotte' in his stories, to whom he devotes an entire chapter ('Ragotte') in *Nos Frères farouches* (1909). His one-act comedy, *Le Plaisir de rompre*, is premiered in March 1897 and dedicated to Edmond Rostand, whose own *Cyrano* will enjoy a box-office success later in the year. Renard's elation is tempered by the suicide of his father who, suffering from a serious disease, shoots himself in the heart. Another one-act play, *Le Pain de ménage*, is given its first performance in 1898.

Despite his increasing fame in Paris, Renard spends more and more time in the country with his family at 'La Gloriette', where he finishes his *Bucoliques* (1898), which describes many of the country folk he knew so well, several of whom appear in the *Histoires naturelles*. It's also at 'La Gloriette' that he adapts *Poil de Carotte* as a play, which is premiered in March 1900 at the Théâtre Antoine in Paris. At one of Sarah Bernhardt's 'Samedis populaires' in Paris, his *Histoires naturelles* are read by Lucien Guitry, to whom he dedicates the 1899 edition, illustrated by Toulouse-Lautrec. On the death of his brother Maurice, Renard returns to Chitry to organize the funeral and arrange the family affairs with his mother and sister. On 6th May he is elected Town Councillor of Chitry. *Poil de Carotte* celebrates its 100th performance in October.

In 1904 Renard is elected Mayor of Chitry. Maurice Ravel composes five of the *Histoires naturelles* in 1906, but Renard does not attend the performance. In 1907 he becomes a member of the Académie Goncourt. In 1909 he finishes his comedy *La Bigote*, which is premiered in October at the Odéon. His mother falls into the garden well at Chitry and is drowned – 'C'est une façon bien compliquée de me faire orphelin,' he notes in his *Journal*. Renard feels prematurely old, and his health begins to fail. At the start of 1910 he is confined to bed, suffering from headaches, stomach-ache, emphysema and arteriosclerosis, his 'maladie de vieux', as he calls it in his correspondence. Despite the floods in Paris, his wife takes him for a walk in Parc Monceau. On 13th February he chairs his final meeting of the county council in Chitry. The effort causes a relapse, and though he rallies, he makes the following note in his journal on 22nd February: 'Aujourd'hui, quarante-six ans. Jusqu'où irai-je? Jusqu'à l'automne?' He dies on 22nd May 1910, and is buried two days later in a civil ceremony at Chitry.

Although the first of the *Histoires naturelles*, 'Le Chasseur d'images', was published in 1895 in *La Nouvelle Revue*, the idea for the volume was born many years previously. When his wife was expecting their first child in 1889, Renard started to write *Poil de Carotte* in his parents' house in Chaumot, and noted in his diary: 'Joindre à ce livre une série sur les animaux: le cochon, sa mort, etc.' ('Follow this book with a series on animals: the pig, his death, etc.') Several of *Poil de Carotte*'s chapter headings anticipate poems from *Histoires naturelles*: 'Les poules', 'Les perdrix', 'Les lapins', 'La taupe', 'La luzerne', 'Le chat', 'Les moutons', 'En chasse', 'La première bécasse', etc.; but whereas the animals in *Poil de Carotte* were viewed from a child's perspective, the *Histoires naturelles* are all observations of a mature poet.

These prose poems were triggered by first-hand experience of the animals, landscape and peasants of Le Morvan, that isolated district of Burgundy where Renard grew up. Yet he is indebted – sometimes to a remarkable degree – to the naturalist Georges-Louis Leclerc, Comte de Buffon (1707–88), whose own *Histoire naturelle* appeared in forty-four volumes between 1749 and 1804, both during his lifetime and posthumously. Renard apostrophizes the great naturalist in 'Turkey-hens': "'Noble turkey-hen,' I say, 'if you were a goose, I would pen your panegyric with one of your quills, as Buffon did. But you are only a turkey-hen.'" He knew Buffon's work intimately and many of the naturalist's phrases appear verbatim in his own *Histoires naturelles*. Buffon, describing the peacock for example, writes how 'son aigrette s'agite sur sa tête', and how the bird seems to take on an 'éclat' of new 'couleurs'. It seems certain that Renard always read the relevant passages in the *Histoire naturelle* before writing his own *Histoires naturelles*. But there is no question of plagiarism. Buffon's style is majestic and sweeping, whereas Renard again and again crystallizes his prose into nuggets of unforgettable poetry, as we see in the way he adapts Buffon's description of the peacock in his own version: 'L'amour avive l'éclat de ses couleurs, et son aigrette tremble comme une lyre' ('Love burnishes the brilliance of his colours, and his crest quivers like a lyre').

Reading *Poil de Carotte*, it becomes clear that Renard as a child spent considerably more time with animals than with his parents. The irony is that he also felt the urge to hunt – a contradiction that is expressed in 'Fish', where M. Vernet is appalled by the torture he inflicts on the gudgeon he has landed, and also at the end of 'The partridges' when Renard, having described the barbarity of the hunt, writes: 'What I deserve is a load of lead up my backside!' And his loathing of the hunt is expressed again and again in his *Journal* and correspondence. On 11th September 1899 he writes to Pottecher: 'Je chasse un peu, mais j'ai un tel écœurement après mes meurtres que ce n'est pas un plaisir sans mélange.' ('I hunt a little, but I feel such revulsion after my murders that it is not unalloyed pleasure.'). And on page 920 of his *Journal* we read: 'Conseil aux chasseurs, de sortir une fois sans leur fusil et de parcourir les champs où ils ont tué…' ('A word of advice for hunters: let them try going out for once without their gun, and let them roam the fields where they have killed…'). No one who reads 'Dédèche Is Dead' or 'The Death of Brunette' can ever doubt Renard's profound love for the creatures he describes.

The eighty-five prose poems that make up Renard's *Histoires naturelles* constantly make us smile at the way he compares animals to human beings. Renard is both poet and humorist. The guinea-fowl is 'the hunchback of my barnyard'; the peacock 'processes with the air of an Indian prince'; the donkey pulls the carriage 'with a civil servant's quick, sharp and mincing step'; the grasshopper is 'the gendarme among insects'; the jay is 'the deputy-prefect of the fields'. Several of the animals are described in no more than a sentence; others are sketched in short prose poems; some, such as 'The Death of Brunette' and 'The Partridges' are short narratives of several pages. Despite this variety of poetic form, Renard imposes a sort of unity on this wonderful work by organizing his poems according to species. After the initial 'Image Hunter', there are farmyard descriptions of hens, cocks, ducks, turkey-hens and guinea-fowls, followed by a poem on pigeons that introduces us to the more picturesque and regal birds: the peacock and the swan. The next section comprises some eighteen poems on what might vaguely be called domestic animals, from dogs, cats and cows to sheep, goats and rabbits. The heart-rending 'Hare' leads into the section on 'wild' creatures: lizards, snakes, weasels, hedgehogs, worms, frogs and toads. Renard then describes such insects as grasshoppers, crickets, cockroaches, glow-worms, spiders, cockchafers, ants, snails, caterpillars, fleas, butterflies, wasps and dragonflies. After an interlude devoted to squirrels, mice, monkeys and stags, he turns his attention to fish (gudgeon, pike and whales) – a section which ends with a moving portrayal of a fisherman who suddenly realizes the cruelty of his sport. As an antidote, we are then introduced to the world of plants (gardens, poppies, vines), before Renard, with undiminished imagination and sensitivity, describes such feathered creatures as bats, canaries, finches, goldfinches, orioles, sparrows, swallows, magpies, blackbirds, parrots, larks, kingfishers (a breathtakingly beautiful poem), sparrow-hawks, wagtails, jays, crows ('a grave accent on the furrow'), partridges and woodcock. The work ends with 'A Family of Trees', 'End of the Hunting Season' and 'New Moon.'

Histoires naturelles, like *Poil de Carotte*, was written over a number of years. Many of the prose-poems appeared in journals and magazines such as *Nouvelle Revue, Echo de Paris, Le Rire, Le Figaro, Gil Blas, La Petite Gironde, L'Auto* and *Paris-Journal*; and some appeared in two of his own works: *Le Vigneron dans sa vigne* (1901) and *Ragotte* (1908). Forty-five of the texts were published by Flammarion in 1896, twenty-two by Floury in 1899; seventy by Flammarion in 1904; eighty-three by Arthème Fayard in 1909; and eighty-five by Bernouard as part of Renard's *Œuvres Complètes* in 1926. When Renard came to revise *Histoires naturelles*, he decided to omit not only all references to actual events and people in the public eye (Gambetta, Coppée, Combes, Ganderax), but also all learned allusions (to Meleager and Aristophanes, for example). The names that remain belong to people and creatures of his acquaintance. Philippe, his trusty servant and factotum; Madame Loriot, mentioned in 'Cocks', the cook in the grand local château; Pointu, one of Renard's dogs; Dédèche, the dog that belonged to his daughter Baïe (its death so upset Renard that he wrote to a friend: 'Nous n'aurons plus jamais de chien'); the cow Brunette, whose death devastated Renard's family. In his *Journal* (p. 853), however, Renard describes the therapeutic way in which writing can overcome sadness: 'Beauté de la littérature. Je perds une vache. J'écris sa mort, et ça me rapporte de quoi acheter une autre vache.' ('The beauty of literature. I lose a cow. I write about its death, and that provides me with the wherewithal to buy another cow.')

'It may be said of almost all works of literature that they are too long', we read in the *Journal*. Renard's own writing, exemplified in *Histoires naturelles*, displays his wonderful gift for compression and distillation. Whereas Balzac, Edmond and Jules Goncourt, Flaubert and Zola painted on a broad canvas, Renard excelled at smaller forms. He observed people and nature at first hand, and recorded what he saw with great precision and an almost total lack of sentimentality. André Gide hit the nail on the head when, writing in his own *Journal* of Renard's *Journal*, he observed that the latter's was 'not a river but a distillery'.

– Richard Stokes, 2010

Monument to Jules Renard in Chitry-les-Mines

Translator's Note

These translations have been made from the Pléiade edition of *Histoires naturelles*, edited by Léon Guichard, which reproduces the text of the 1909 edition, published by Arthème Fayard. 'Nouvelle lune' from *Ragotte* is printed as an appendix.

I would like to thank Florence Daguerre de Hureaux, Elisabeth and Bruno Reyre, Françoise Clerc, Laure Brissaud and Lucinda Rogers for their invaluable suggestions and advice.

Histoires
naturelles

The Image Hunter

He jumps out of bed early in the morning and sets out only if his mind is clear, his heart pure, his body light as a summer shirt. He carries no provisions. He will drink the fresh air en route and breathe in the healthy smells. He leaves all his weapons at home and simply keeps his eyes open. His eyes will serve as nets where images will be trapped.

The first to be snared is the road with its bones, polished pebbles and the popped veins of its ruts, between two hedges laden with sloes and mulberries.

Next he captures the river. Sallow at the bends, it sleeps beneath the willow's caress. It glistens when a fish turns up its belly, as if someone had thrown in a coin, and as soon as it starts to drizzle, the river has gooseflesh.

He gathers the image of waving wheat, appetizing lucerne and fields hemmed by streams. He seizes in passing the flight of a lark or a goldfinch.

Then he enters the wood. He had no idea his senses were so receptive. Quickly drenched in perfumes, he does not miss the slightest murmur, and, to communicate with the trees, his veins mingle with the veins of the leaves.

Soon, quivering to the point of discomfort, he perceives too much, he is agitated, he is frightened, he leaves the wood and follows from afar the peasant woodcutters returning to the village.

Outside, he stares for a moment until his eyes blaze at the setting sun, as on the horizon it sheds its luminous raiment, its scattered clouds.

Home at last, his head brimming, he turns off his lamp and, before falling asleep, takes great pleasure in counting up all the images he has caught.

Obediently, they reappear as his memory summons them. Each one wakens another, and the phosphorescent throng multiplies with newcomers, just as partridges, hunted and dispersed all day long, sing in the evening, sheltered from danger, and call to one another from their deep furrows.

The Hen

Feet together, she jumps down from the coop, as soon as the door is opened.

A common hen, modestly attired, she has never laid a golden egg.

Blinded by the light, she takes a few hesitant steps in the barnyard.

First of all she sees the heap of ashes, where each morning she frolics.

She rolls in it, wallows in it, and, with a swift flutter of wings, she puffs up her feathers and shakes off the night's fleas.

Then she goes and drinks from the shallow dish the shower has just filled.

Water is all she ever drinks.

She drinks in little sips, straightening her neck and balancing on the edge of the dish.

Then she hunts around for her scattered food.

Hers are the delicate herbs, the insects and the stray seeds.

Tirelessly, she pecks and pecks.

Occasionally, she stops.

Upright beneath her Phrygian cap, bright-eyed, jabot displayed to advantage, she listens, first with one ear, then the other.

And, convinced nothing has happened, she renews her search.

She raises her stiff feet high in the air, as though she had gout. She spreads her toes and sets them down carefully, without a sound.

As if she were walking barefoot.

Cocks

I

He has never crowed. He has never spent a night in a henhouse or known a single hen.

He is made out of wood, with an iron leg protruding from his stomach, and he has lived, for years and years, on top of an old church, the like of which no one dares build any more. It resembles a barn, and the ridge of its tiled roof is as straight as an ox's back.

And now some masons appear at the other end of the church.

The wooden cock looks at them, until a gust of wind compels him to turn his back.

And, each time he whirls back round, new stones block off a little more of his horizon.

Soon, raising his head with a jerk, he notices, on the top of the steeple they've just completed, a young cockerel that was not there in the morning. This stranger carries his tail high, opens his beak like a singer, and, wings on hips, brand-new, glistens in the sunlight.

At first, the two cocks compete to see who can move faster. But the old wooden cock is soon exhausted and surrenders. Under his one-and-only foot, the roof beam threatens to collapse. He leans stiffly, ready to fall. He creaks and stops.

And here come the carpenters.

They demolish this worm-eaten corner of the church, take down the cock and parade him through the village. Anyone can touch him, for a fee.

Some give an egg, others a sou, and Mme Loriot gives a silver coin.

The carpenters have a drink or two, and, after quarrelling about who should have the cock, they decide to burn him.

They build him a nest of sticks and straw, and then set fire to it.

The wooden cock crackles brightly, and his flames rise up to heaven, which he has richly deserved and reached.[1]

II

Each morning, jumping from his perch, the cock looks to see if the other one's still there – and the other one always is.

The cock can boast of having defeated all his earthly rivals, but the other cock is always there, invincible, out of reach.

The cock crows over and over again: he calls, he provokes, he threatens – but the other only replies in his own good time, and initially not at all.

The cock preens himself, puffs out his feathers, which are not unimpressive: some blue, some silvery – but the other one, against the blue sky, glitters with gold.

The cock gathers his hens together, and marches at their head. Observe: they belong to him; they all love him and they all fear him – but the other one is worshipped by swallows.

---

1 '*Le ciel qu'il a bien gagné*'. Renard plays on the verb '*gagner*' – 'to merit', 'to reach'.

The cock struts about. Now and again he utters his amorous grace notes, and scores many little triumphs with his shrill tones, but the other one is actually getting married and chimes out his village wedding with all the bells ringing.

The jealous cock sharpens his spurs for the ultimate battle; his tail looks like a cloak draped over a sword. His crest bursting with blood, he defies all the cocks of heaven – but the other one, who's not frightened to face even hurricanes, is at this moment playing with the breeze, and turns his back.

And the cock becomes more and more desperate until the day is ended.

One by one his hens go home. He is left alone, hoarse, exhausted, in the now darkening yard – while the other one, resplendent in the last rays of the sun, sings with his pure voice the peaceful evening angelus.

Ducks

I

The duck walks in front, limping with both feet, to dabble in the pot-hole she knows so well.

The drake follows her. Wing-tips folded across his back, he also limps with both feet.

Duck and drake walk on in silence, as though to a business meeting.

The duck is first to slip into the muddy water littered with feathers, droppings, a vine leaf and straw. She has almost disappeared.

She is waiting. She is ready.

And the drake enters in turn. He submerges his rich colours. All you see of him is his green head and the kiss-curl of his derrière. Both feel at home there. The water warms. It is never drained, and only ever renewed when there's a thunderstorm.

The drake, with his flattened beak, nibbles and squeezes the duck's neck. For a moment he splashes about and the water is so thick that there's hardly a ripple. Quickly calm and smooth again, it reflects, in black, a patch of cloudless sky.

Duck and drake no longer move. The sun bakes them and lulls them to sleep. You could come quite close and not notice them. Their presence is only revealed by the occasional bubble that bursts on the stagnant surface.

II

Both are sleeping outside the closed door, side by side and flat on the ground, like the clogs of a neighbour who visits an invalid.

Turkey-Hens

I

She struts through the barnyard, as though she were living under the *ancien régime.*

The other fowl do nothing but eat, at all hours and no matter what. She, though, has regular meals, and in between is concerned only with looking her best. All her feathers are starched, and the tips of her wings score lines on the earth, as though to trace the path she wishes to take: she will walk *here* and nowhere else.

She carries her head too high ever to see her feet.

She distrusts no one, and, as soon as I approach, she imagines I have come to pay my respects.

She's already gobbling with pride.

'Noble turkey-hen,' I say, 'if you were a goose, I would pen your panegyric with one of your quills, as Buffon did. But you are only a turkey-hen.'

I must have provoked her, for blood rushes to her head. Grapes of wrath hang from her beak. She sees red. With a sharp click, she opens the fan of her tail, and this old crosspatch turns her back on me.

II

Out on the road, here they are again – a whole boarding-school of turkey-hens.

Every day, whatever the weather, they go for a walk.

They fear neither the rain – nobody knows better than a turkey-hen how to tuck up a skirt – nor the sun, a turkey-hen never goes out without a parasol.

The Guinea-Fowl

She is the hunchback of my barnyard. She dreams only of wounds, because of her hump.

The hens say nothing to her: suddenly, she swoops and harries them.

Then she lowers her head, leans forward, and, with all the speed her skinny legs can muster, runs and strikes with her hard beak at the very centre of a turkey's tail.

This poseur was provoking her.

Thus, with her bluish head and raw wattles, pugnaciously she rages from morn to night. She fights for no reason, perhaps because she always thinks they are making fun of her figure, her bald head and drooping tail.

And she never stops screaming her discordant cry, which pierces the air like a needle.

Sometimes she leaves the yard and vanishes. She gives the peace-loving poultry a moment's respite. But she returns more rowdy and shrill. And in a frenzy she wallows in the earth.

Whatever's wrong with her?

The cunning creature is playing a trick.

She went to lay her egg in the open country.

I can look for it if I like.

And she rolls in the dust, like a hunchback.

The Goose

Like the other village girls, Tiennette would like to go to Paris. But is she even capable of minding her geese?

For really, she follows rather than leads them. She does her knitting, mechanically, behind her flock, and relies on the Toulouse goose, who's as sensible as any grown-up.

The Toulouse goose knows the way, knows where good grass can be found and when it's time to go home.

As full of courage as the gander is devoid of it, she protects her sisters from the vicious dog. Her neck pulsates and snakes along the ground, then draws itself up – and she tyrannizes the frightened Tiennette. As soon as everything's under control, she sings triumphantly through her nose, indicating who's responsible for keeping order.

She has no doubt she could do even better.

And one evening, she leaves the region. She waddles down the road, beak to wind, feathers pressed flat. The women she passes don't dare stop her. She walks at a frightening pace.

And while Tiennette, who stays behind, grows more and more stupid and indistinguishable from all her geese, the Toulouse goose arrives in Paris.

The Pigeons

I

Even though they make a sound like muffled drums on the roof;

Even though they emerge from the shade, tumble, explode into the sunshine and return to the shade;

Even though the evanescent colour of their throats flushes and fades like an opal on the finger;

Even though they fall asleep at night in the woods, huddled so closely together that the topmost branch of the oak threatens to break beneath its load of painted fruit;

Even though these two exchange frenzied greetings and, one after the other, break into sudden convulsions;

Even though one of them returns from afar, with a letter, and comes flying like the thoughts of a distant loved one (Ah! A pledge!) –

All these pigeons, who seem entertaining at first, turn out to be bores.

They don't know how to stay put, and travel simply hasn't broadened their horizon.

All their lives they remain a little stupid. They persist in thinking that babies are made through the beak.

And in the long run you cannot stand their hereditary mania for always having something stuck in their gullets.

II

THE TWO PIGEONS: Come, my grrross one, come, my grrross one, come, my grrross one…

The Peacock

He will surely get married today.

It was to have been yesterday. In full regalia he was ready. It was only his bride he was waiting for. She has not come. She cannot be long.

Proudly he processes with the air of an Indian prince, bearing about his person the customary lavish gifts.

Love burnishes the brilliance of his colours, and his crest quivers like a lyre.

His bride does not appear.

He climbs to the top of the roof and looks towards the sun. He utters his devilish cry:

Léon! Léon!

It is thus that he summons his bride. He can see nothing drawing near, and no one replies. The fowls are used to all this and do not even raise their heads. They are tired of admiring him. He descends once more to the yard, so sure of his beauty that he is incapable of bitterness.

His marriage will take place tomorrow.

And, not knowing what to do for the rest of the day, he heads for the flight of steps. He ascends them, as though they were the steps of a temple, with a formal tread.

He lifts his train, heavy with the eyes that have been unable to free themselves from it.

Once more he repeats the ceremony.

The Swan

He glides on the pond like a white sledge, from cloud to cloud. For he is hungry only for the fleecy clouds that he sees forming, moving, dissolving in the water. It is one of these that he wants. He takes aim with his beak and suddenly immerses his snow-clad neck.

Then, like a woman's arm emerging from a sleeve, he draws it back up.

He has caught nothing.

He looks about: the startled clouds have vanished.

Only for a second is he disappointed, for the clouds are not slow to return, and, over there, where the ripples fade, there is one reappearing.

Gently, on his soft cushion of down, the swan paddles and approaches...

He exhausts himself fishing for empty reflections, and perhaps he will die, a victim of that illusion, before catching a single shred of cloud.

But what am I saying?

Each time he dives, he burrows with his beak in the nourishing mud and brings up a worm.

He's getting as fat as a goose.

The Dog

We can't put Pointu outside in weather like this. The wind is whistling so icily under the door that he's even compelled to leave the doormat. He looks for something better and gently pushes his friendly head between our chairs. But we're sitting huddled together, elbow to elbow, round the fire, and I give Pointu a slap. My father pushes him away with his foot. Mother calls him names. My sister offers him an empty glass.

Pointu sneezes and goes out to the kitchen to see if we're there.

Then he comes back, forcing a way into the circle at the risk of getting strangled by knees, and finally moves to a corner of the fireplace.

After turning round and round for a long time in the same place, he sits down next to the andiron and doesn't stir. He looks so sweetly at his masters that we let him be. But the almost red-hot andiron and the scattered ashes burn his backside.

He stays put, all the same.

We create a gap for him to pass through.

'Beat it, stupid!'

But he doesn't budge. At the hour when the teeth of all stray dogs are chattering with cold, Pointu, warm as toast, his fur scorched, his hindquarters roasted, holds back his howls and smiles a sickly smile, his eyes full of tears.

The Dogs

The two dogs rutting over there on the other side of the canal, which Gloriette and I couldn't help watching from our bench, presented us with a grotesque and painful scene which dragged on and on, until Coursol approached. He was bringing home his sheep along the canal, carrying on his shoulder a log that he had picked up on the way to keep himself warm in winter.

As soon as he saw that one of the two dogs was his own, he seized it by the collar and began without haste to beat the other with the log.

Since the two animals could not be separated, Coursol, surrounded by his sheep, had to hit harder. The dog howled and could not break free. You could hear the blows of the log resounding on the animal's spine.

'Poor beasts,' said Gloriette, as white as a sheet.

'That's how they treat them in the country,' I said, 'and the wonder is that Coursol doesn't throw them into the canal. Water would do the job quicker.'

'What a monster!' said Gloriette.

'Not at all! That's Coursol. He's a good, peace-loving man.'

Gloriette held back her tears. It made me sick as much as her, but I was used to it.

'Tell him to stop!' said Gloriette.

'He's too far away to hear properly.'

'Stand up! Wave to him!'

'If he could hear me, he'd reply without anger: "Would you have me leave the dogs as they are?"'

As Gloriette looked on, utterly pale and with open mouth, Coursol continued to rain down blows on the aching animal.

'This is gruesome! If I were to leave, you could confront this villain better on your own!' said Gloriette, suddenly embarrassed.

I was going to give some sort of reply, such as: 'But it's outside our parish!', when a final blow of the log, hard enough to fell them both, separated the two animals. Coursol, having acted as he had to, drove his sheep on towards the village. The dogs, free at last, remained for a few moments next to each other. Shamefaced, they started to sniff each other, still joined through memory.

Dédèche Is Dead

He was Mademoiselle's little terrier and we all loved him.

He knew the art of curling himself up into a ball, anywhere, and even on a table he seemed to sleep in the hollow of a nest.

He understood that caresses with his tongue had become disagreeable to us, and he now only offered his paw, delicately, to our cheeks. We just had to protect our eyes.

He used to laugh. We thought for a long time that it was a way of sneezing, but it really was a laugh.

Although he was never deeply depressed, he knew how to cry, that's to say grunt from the throat, with a drop of pure water in the corner of his eyes.

He sometimes managed to get lost and find his way home all by himself, so intelligently, that we would try to add several expressions of esteem to our cries of joy.

He could not, of course, speak, despite our efforts. It was in vain that Mademoiselle used to say: 'Couldn't you just speak a tiny bit!'

He would look at her, quivering, astonished as much as she. He gestured clearly with his tail, he opened his jaws, but without barking. He guessed that Mademoiselle hoped for more than a bark, and the words were right next to his heart, ready to rise to his tongue and his lips. Eventually he would utter them, but he was not yet old enough!

One evening without moonlight, in the countryside, as Dédèche was looking for his friends by the roadside, a large dog that no one recognized and almost certainly belonged to a poacher, seized this fragile ball of silk, shook it, strangled it, discarded it and ran off.

Ah! If Mademoiselle could have seized this ferocious dog, bitten its neck, rolled it in the dust and suffocated it!

Dédèche recovered from the fang wounds but his haunches were weakened and sore.

He began to piss everywhere. Outside, he pissed like a pump, as much as he could, happy to free us from worry, but almost as soon as he came back inside, he could not restrain himself. As soon as you turned your back, he turned his against the leg of a table or chair, and Mademoiselle uttered her mechanical cry of alarm: 'A sponge! Some water! Some sulphur!'

We grew angry, scolded Dédèche in a terrible voice, beat him with violent gestures that never touched him – his sensitive gaze replied: 'I know, but what can I do?'

He remained friendly and gracious, but sometimes he arched his back, as if he felt the teeth of the poacher's dog in his spine.

And then his smell finally prompted our friends to insult him most unwittily.

Even Mademoiselle's heart began to harden!

Dédéche had to be killed.

It was simple: make an incision in a mouthful of meat, insert two types of powder, one potassium cyanide, the other tartaric acid, sew the pellet up with very fine thread. First give him an innocuous portion, as a game, then the real one. The stomach digests, and the two powders react together, creating hydrocyanic or prussic acid, which destroys the animal.

I do not now wish to remember which of us gave him the pellets.

Dédèche waits, stretched out, very well-behaved, in his basket. And we also wait, we listen in the adjoining room, slumped in our chairs, as if overcome with immense fatigue.

Fifteen minutes pass, thirty. Someone says gently:

'I'll take a look.'

'Another five minutes!'

Our ears boom. Wasn't that the distant howl of a dog we could hear, the poacher's dog?

At last, the bravest of us disappears and returns to say in an unrecognizable voice:

'It's all over!'

Mademoiselle lays her head on the bed and sobs. She sobs without control, just as people laugh hysterically, when they only wish to laugh.

She keeps saying, her face in the pillow:

'No, no, I shan't drink my chocolate this morning!'

To her mother, who talks about getting her a husband, she mutters that she will remain a spinster.

The others hold back their tears, just in time. They all feel that they could weep, and that each new fount would cause another to gush forth.

They say to Mademoiselle:

'Don't be silly, it's nothing!'

Why nothing? That was a life, and we've no idea what that life, which we've just destroyed, would have become. Embarrassed, and in order not to acknowledge that the death of a little dog could distress us so, we think of humans that had died, or that might die, think of all that is mysterious, incomprehensible, black and cold.

The culprit tells himself: 'I've just committed a treacherous murder.'

He rises to his feet and dares to gaze on his victim. We later discover that he kissed Dédèche's sweet little skull that was still warm.

'Were his eyes open?'

'Yes, but they were glassy, and could not see.'

'Did he die without pain?'

'Ah yes, I'm sure he did.'

'Without a struggle?'

'He merely stretched out his little paw to the edge of the basket, as if it to shake hands.'

The Cat

I

Mine doesn't eat mice; he doesn't care for them. He only catches them to play with. When he's finished playing, he spares its life, and goes off to dream elsewhere, the harmless creature, seated in the loop of his tail, head closed tight like a fist.

But because of those claws, the mouse is dead.

II

We tell him: 'Catch the mice and leave the birds!'

A very subtle difference, and even the cleverest cat can sometimes make mistakes.

The Cow

I

Tired of searching for one, we ended up giving her no name at all. She's simply called 'the cow', and that's the name which suits her best.

Besides, what does it matter, provided she eats!

And now she has everything she wants, fresh grass, hay, vegetables, grain and even bread and salt – she eats everything, all the time, twice over, since she chews her cud.

As soon as she sees me, she trots up on her split hooves, her hide stretched over her legs like a white stocking, convinced that I'm bringing her something to eat. And admiring her each time, all I can say is: 'Come on, eat this!'

But from what she absorbs, she makes milk, not fat. At the appointed hour she offers her full, square udder. She does not hold back her milk – there are cows that do – generously, through her four elastic teats, hardly squeezed, she empties her reservoir. She moves neither foot nor tail, but with her supple, enormous tongue she loves to lick the milkmaid's back.

Although she lives alone, her appetite prevents her from getting bored. Only rarely does she let out a sad low, in vague remembrance of her last calf. But she likes visitors, and receives then graciously with her horns held high and with a thread of water and a wisp of hay dangling from her avid lips.

The men, who fear nothing, stroke her swollen belly; the women, astonished that so vast an animal could be so gentle, now only shrink from her kisses, and dream happy dreams.

II

She likes me to scratch her between her horns. I draw back a little, because she moves forward with pleasure, and the good creature lets me continue till I tread in her cowpat.

The Death of Brunette

Philippe wakes me, saying that he got up in the night to listen, and that her breathing was calm.

But since this morning, he's been worried about her.

He gives her hay and she refuses it.

He offers her a little fresh grass, and Brunette, usually so fond of delicacies, hardly touches it. She no longer looks at her calf and doesn't like it nuzzling her when he gets up on his stiff legs to suck.

Philippe separates them and ties up the calf away from its mother. Brunette doesn't seem to notice.

Philippe's anxiety affects us all. Even the children want to get up.

The vet arrives, examines Brunette and leads her out of the barn. She knocks against the wall and stumbles over the threshold. She almost falls; we have to take her back in.

'She's very sick,' says the vet.

We daren't ask what's wrong with her.

He fears it's milk fever, which is often fatal, especially with good milkers, and recalling one by one all those cows he thought he had lost but managed to save, he takes a little bottle and with a brush spreads the liquid over Brunette's flanks.

'It will act as a vesicatory,' he says. 'I don't know the exact formula. It comes from Paris. If the infection doesn't reach the brain, she'll

40

get over it by herself; otherwise, I'll use the iced-water method. It comes as a surprise to simple peasants, but I know what I'm talking about.'

'Go ahead, Monsieur.'

Brunette, lying on the straw, can still hold up her head. She stops chewing the cud. She seems to be holding her breath in order to hear what's going on inside her.

We wrap her in a woollen blanket, because her ears and horns are growing cold.

'As long as her ears don't droop,' Philippe says, 'there's hope.'

Twice she tries in vain to stand up. She breathes heavily, at ever longer intervals.

And then she lets her head droop onto her left flank.

'Things are getting worse,' Philippe says, crouching beside her and calling her pet names.

She raises her head and lowers it onto the edge of the manger, so heavily that the muffled sound makes us cry out.

We surround Brunette with heaps of straw so she won't hurt herself.

She stretches out her neck and legs, lies down, spreads herself to her full length, as she used to do in the field when a storm was brewing.

The vet decides to bleed her. He does not come too close. He's as knowledgeable as anyone, but is considered less brave than some.

At the first taps of the wooden mallet, the lancet slides over the vein. After a more confident blow, blood spurts out into the tin pail that milk usually fills to the brim.

To stop the flow, the vet inserts a steel pin into the vein.

Then, from Brunette's head to her tail, we apply a sheet wet with well water, and change it frequently because it heats up so quickly.

She doesn't even shiver. Philippe holds her firmly by the horns and prevents her head from banging against her left flank.

Brunette, as though tamed, no longer moves. We can't tell whether she's getting better or worse.

We are all sad, but Philippe's sadness has the mournfulness of an animal watching another animal suffer.

His wife brings him his morning soup which he eats without appetite, sitting on a stool, and which he doesn't finish.

'It's the end,' he says, 'Brunette's body is swelling!'

At first we don't believe him, but Philippe is right. Brunette swells as we watch, and the swelling does not subside, as though the air that enters can't get out.

Philippe's wife asks:

'Is she dead?'

'Can't you see?' Philippe says harshly.

Mme. Philippe goes out into the farmyard.

'I shan't go looking for another in a hurry,' Philippe says.

'Another what?'

'Another Brunette.'

'You'll go when I want you to,' I say in a tone of authority that startles me.

We try to make ourselves believe that the whole business is more irritating than painful, and already we're saying that Brunette has snuffed it.

But that evening when I met the church bell-ringer, I don't know what kept me from saying:

'Here are a hundred sous, go and ring the passing-bell for someone who's died in my house.'

The Ox

I

The door opens this morning, as usual, and Castor, without stumbling, leaves the stable. In slow draughts he drinks his share of the trough water, leaving the rest for the late-comer, Pollux. Then, muzzle dripping like a tree after a downpour, he walks, willingly, ponderously, methodically, to his usual place under the wagon's yoke.

Horns tied, head motionless, he wrinkles his belly, swishes lazily with his tail at the black flies and, like a maid dozing on her broom, chews the cud while waiting for Pollux.

In the farmyard, however, the bustling servants shout and swear, and the dog yaps, as though scenting a stranger's approach.

Could this be docile Pollux who, resisting the goad for the first time in his life, keeps wandering around, bumping into Castor, steaming and, though harnessed, still tries to shake off the yoke they share?

No, it's another one.

Castor, separated from Pollux, stops chewing when he sees, close to, the bleary eye of a bull he does not recognize.

II

As the sun sets, the oxen slowly drag through the fields the light plough of their shadow.

The Bull

I

The fisherman with his rod moves lightly along the banks of the River Yonne, casting his green fly over the water.

He catches the green flies on the trunks of poplars that have been polished by cattle rubbing against them.

He casts his line with a sharp snap, and reels it in with authority.

He deludes himself that each new spot is the best, and soon abandons it, stepping over a stile and passing from one field to the next.

Suddenly, while crossing a large, sun-baked field, he stops.

Over there, in the midst of peaceful, reclining cows, the bull has just heaved itself to its feet.

It's a notorious bull, whose huge size amazes people passing on the road. He is admired from a distance, and, if he hasn't already done so, could hurl a man into the air, like an arrow, with the bow of his horns. Gentler than a lamb, when the mood takes him, he is prone to sudden fits of rage, and if you are nearby, you never know what might happen.

The fisherman observes him out of the corner of his eye.

'If I run,' he thinks, 'the bull will be upon me before I get out of the field. If I jump into the river, unable to swim I'll drown. If I lie down and play dead, they say the bull will sniff me and leave me alone.

How can they be sure? And suppose he doesn't go away! Better to deceive him and pretend I don't care.'

And the fisherman continues to fish as if the bull were not there. In this way he hopes to outwit him.

Beneath his straw hat the nape of his neck is burning.

He controls his feet that are itching to run, and compels them to saunter across the grass. Heroically, he casts his green fly on the water.

But why this haste?

The bull ignores him and stays with the cows.

He only stood up to stretch his legs, out of weariness, the way one stretches one's limbs.

He turns his frizzy head to the evening breeze.

He bellows intermittently, eyes half-closed.

He lows listlessly, and listens to his lowing.

II

Women know him by his frizzy forehead.

III

'How he stares at me!'

'Don't be frightened, Gloriette, he can see that you're a good woman.'

The Water-Flies

There's only one oak tree in the middle of the field, and the cows occupy all the shade of its leaves.

With lowered heads, they mockingly point two horns at the sun.

They'd be fine if it weren't for the flies.

But today, my word, they're voracious. Pungent and abundant, the black ones cling like a film of soot to the eyes, the nostrils, even to the corners of the mouth, and the green ones, by preference, suck at the most recent scratch.

When a cow's leather apron moves, or she pounds the dry earth with her hoof, the swarm of flies changes position with a murmur. As if they were fermenting.

It's so hot that the old women, on their doorsteps, sense the storm and start to joke a little:

'Watch out for the thunder,' they say.

In the distance, a luminous spear pierces the sky, noiselessly. A drop of rain falls.

The cows, alerted, raise their heads, move right up to the oak and, patiently, snort.

They know: the good flies will now come and drive away the bad.

Infrequent at first, one by one, then in dense swarms, all together, they fall from the lacerated sky onto the enemy, who gradually withdraw, dwindle and disperse.

Soon, from flat nose to indestructible tail, the streaming cows ripple with pleasure beneath the victorious swarm of water-flies.

The Mare

Harvest time. The barns brim with hay right up to the roof-tiles. Men and women are hurrying, because the weather looks threatening– and if the rain were to fall on the harvested hay it would lose its value. All the hay-wagons are on the move: one's being loaded, another drawn by horses to the farm. Night has fallen, and still the wagons come and go.

A mare whinnies rebelliously between the shafts. She is answering her foal who has been calling her, having spent the day in the fields without slaking his thirst.

She feels that the day is done, that she can now rejoin her foal, and she pulls at her collar, as if she alone were harnessed. The wagon comes to a standstill by the wall of the barn. They unyoke her, and the freed mare would have lumbered to the gate where her foal was sniffing the air, had they not stopped her, because she had to go back again and fetch the final wagon.

The Horse

My horse is not handsome. He has too many knots and hollows, flat sides, a rat's tail and an Englishwoman's buck-teeth. But he moves me. I can't get over the fact that he remains in my service and allows himself, without rebelling, to be turned this way and that.

Each time I put on his harness, I expect him to tell me *No*, with a sudden gesture, and bolt.

He does nothing of the sort. He lowers and lifts his huge head as though to straighten a hat, and steps back submissively between the shafts.

And so I'm generous with his oats and corn. I brush him till his coat shines like a cherry. I comb his mane, I braid his scrawny tail. I caress him with my hands and my voice. I sponge his eyes and wax his hooves.

Does that mean anything to him?

No one knows.

He farts.

I admire him most when he pulls me along in the carriage. I whip him and he breaks into a trot. I shout *whoa*! and he stops. I pull the rein to the left and he goes to the left, instead of going to the right and dumping me somewhere in the ditch and kicking out at me.

He frightens me, shames me and arouses my pity.

Will he not soon wake up from his half-sleep and, imperiously usurping my place, demote me to his?

What is he thinking about?

He farts, farts, farts.

The Donkey

I

It's all the same to him. Each morning, with a civil servant's quick, sharp and mincing step, he pulls Jacquot the carrier's wagon, as he distributes from village to village articles purchased in town: groceries, bread, butcher's meat, a few newspapers, a letter.

Having done the rounds, Jacquot and the donkey work for themselves. The wagon becomes a cart. They go together to the vineyards, to the wood, to the potato fields. They bring back vegetables or green brushwood or something else, depending on the day.

Jacquot keeps saying '*Gee up! Gee up!*' without any reason, as though he were snoring. Sometimes the donkey, because of a thistle he smells or a sudden idea, stops walking. Jacquot puts an arm round his neck and pushes. If the donkey resists, Jacquot bites his ear.

They eat in roadside ditches, the master a crust of bread and onions, the animal whatever he wants.

Night has fallen by the time they reach home. Their shadows move slowly from one tree to the next.

Suddenly the lake of silence, in which all things are bathed, is split apart.

What housewife can at this hour be drawing full buckets of water from her well, by turning a rusty, screeching winch?

It's the donkey returning home, braying himself hoarse, saying he couldn't care less, he couldn't care less.

II

Donkey: a rabbit writ large.

The Hog

Grumpy, but familiar as though we had grown up together, you stick your snout everywhere, and walk with it as much as with your feet.

You hide your tiny blackcurrant eyes beneath beetroot-leaf ears.

Your belly's as big as a gooseberry.

You have the same long hair, the same light skin, and a short curly tail.

And nasty people say: 'You dirty pig!'

They say that, if nothing disgusts you, you disgust everyone, and that you only like to drink greasy dishwater.

That's slander.

If they wash you, you'll look fine.

It's their fault if you neglect yourself.

Since they make your bed, you lie in it, and dirtiness only comes second nature to you.

The Swine and the Pearls

As soon as we let him into the meadow, the porker starts eating and his snout never leaves the ground.

He does not select the best grass. He attacks whatever's nearest and pushes his unflagging nose in front of him like a ploughshare or a blind mole.

His only concern is to fill out a belly that already looks like a salting tub, and he never bothers about the weather.

What matter if his bristles almost caught fire just now in the noonday sun, or if a heavy, hail-swollen cloud bursts above the meadow?

The magpie, of course, escapes in her mechanical flight; the turkey-hens hide in the hedge, the boyish colt shelters beneath an oak.

But the porker stays put where he's eating.

He doesn't miss a mouthful.

He doesn't even wiggle his tail.

Riddled with hailstones, he hardly has time to grunt:

'More of their beastly pearls!'

The Sheep

I

They're returning from the fields of stubble, where they've been grazing since morning, noses in their bodies' shade.

A sign from the lazy shepherd – and the indispensable dog attacks the flock on the required flank.

The flock fills the whole road, undulates from one ditch to the other and overflows; or, crammed together, forming a single downy mass, tramples the ground with the tiny steps of old women. When the flock starts to run, the hooves sound like rushes, and riddle the dust of the road with honeycombs.

This curly sheep, with its thick fleece, bounces like a bundle hurled in the air, and pastilles spill from its cornet-shaped ear.

This one has vertigo, and his knee bangs against his head that's been badly screwed on.

They invade the village. Today must be their holiday, for they're bleating irrepressibly and joyfully through the streets.

But they don't stop in the village, and I see them reappear further off. They reach the horizon. Over the hill they climb, as light as air, up towards the sun. They draw near and lie down at a distance.

Stragglers, silhouetted against the sky, take on one final unexpected shape, and rejoin the huddled flock.

A tuft of wool comes loose again, floats like white foam, becomes smoke, then steam, then nothing.

A single foot sticks out of the flock.

The flock grows longer, tapers, like wool on a spindle, to infinity.

The shivering sheep fall asleep around the weary sun, which unfastens its crown and sticks its rays in their wool, until tomorrow dawns.

II

THE SHEEP: Bu-u-ut... Bu-u-ut... Bu-u-ut...

THE SHEEPDOG: No buts about it!

The Nanny-Goat

No one reads the page from the official newspaper displayed on the wall of the town hall.

Except the nanny-goat.

She stands up on her hind legs, leans her forelegs below the poster, shakes her horns and her beard, and moves her head from right to left, like an old woman reading.

Having read the page, with its delicious smell of fresh glue, the goat eats it.

Nothing is wasted in our town.

The Billy-Goat

His smell precedes him. He's not yet in sight but *it* has arrived.

He leads the herd and the sheep follow, pell-mell, in a cloud of dust.

His coat is long and dry and parted down the back.

He's less proud of his beard than his height, for the nanny-goat also wears a beard beneath her chin.

When he passes, some people hold their noses, others enjoy that smell.

He looks neither to the right nor the left: he walks stiffly, ears pointed, tail short. If mankind has burdened him with their sins, he knows nothing of it, and, solemnly, releases a rosary of dung.

He's called Alexandre, a name known even to the dogs.

When the day is done and the sun set, he returns to the village with the harvesters, and his horns, drooping with age, gradually take on the curved shape of sickles.

The Rabbits

In their hutch made from half a barrel, Lenoir and Legris, paws warm beneath their fur, eat like cows. They have only one meal which lasts all day.

If you're slow to toss them a fresh weed, they gnaw the old one down to the root, and even the root keeps their teeth busy.

Now a head of lettuce has come their way. Together, Lenoir and Legris set to work.

Nose to nose they toil away, heads nodding, ears trotting.

When only one leaf is left, they each take an end and see who can eat faster.

You'd think that they were playing, except they don't laugh, and that, once the leaf was devoured, a fraternal caress would bring their snouts together.

But Legris is weakening. Since yesterday, he's had a swollen belly, bloated by a water pocket. As a matter of fact, he's been over-indulging. Though a lettuce leaf should slip down easily enough, even on a full stomach, he can't go on. He drops the leaf and lies down on his side, on top of his droppings, suffering short spasms.

There he lies, rigid, feet apart, like a gunsmith's advertisement: *A clean shot.*

Surprised, Lenoir stops eating for a moment. Standing on his hind legs, breathing gently, lips together, eyes pink-rimmed, he stares.

He looks like a wizard fathoming a mystery.

His two erect ears mark the supreme moment.

Then they fall back.

And he finishes the lettuce leaf.

The Hare

Philippe had promised to show me a hare in its seat. It's difficult, you need eyes like the old hunters had.

We cross a field of stubble, protected from the North Wind by a hillside.

A hare in the morning takes shelter in its home from the gusting wind, and even if the wind turns in the course of the day, the hare stays in its seat till nightfall.

When hunting, I look at the dog, the trees, the larks, the sky; Philippe looks at the ground. He peers into every furrow, downhill and uphill. A stone, a clod of earth attracts his attention. A hare, perhaps? He goes to check.

And this time, there is one!

'Do you want to shoot it?' Philippe asks me in a restrained manner.

I turn round. Philippe, motionless, staring at a single spot on the ground, stands there, gun at the ready.

'Can you see it?' he says.

'Where?'

'Can't you see its eyes move?'

'No.'

'There, in front of you.'

'In the furrow?'

'Yes, but not in the first, the other one.'

'I can't see anything.'

I rub my blurred eyes in vain. Philippe, pale from the excitement of spotting the hare, repeats:

'You can't see it? You really can't see it?!'

And his hands are quivering. He fears the hare will make off.

'Point it out,' I say, 'with your gun.'

'Look, there – you can see the eye, his eye, at the end of the barrel!'

'It's no use! I can see nothing; take aim, Philippe, take aim!'

I place myself behind Philippe and, even using the sights of his gun, I can't see it!

It's infuriating!

I see something, but it can't be the hare; it's a lump of earth, yellow like all the clods in the stubble field. I search for its eye. There is no eye.

I resist telling Philippe:

'It doesn't matter, shoot!'

And the dog, which had been running in the distance, returns to our side. As there is no wind, he cannot smell the hare, but he might rush off at random. Beneath his breath, Philippe threatens to slap and kick him, if he moves.

Philippe no longer talks to me. He has done the impossible, and waits for me to give up.

Ah! where is this eye, large, round and black, resembling a little plum, this eye of a terrorized hare, where is it?

Ah! I see it!

As I shoot, the hare hurtles out of its seat, its head shattered. And it was indeed the hare that I had seen. I had seen it almost immediately, I have sharp eyes. I had been deceived by the hare's pose. I had expected it to be rolled up like a ball, like a young dog, and I had been looking for the eye in the ball. But the hare had been lying down to its full length, its forelegs joined together and its ears turned down. He only makes a hole for his rump, in order to be as near as possible on a level with the stubble. His rump is here, his eye there. Hence my brief hesitation.

It's cowardly to kill a hare in its seat, I say to Philippe. We ought to have thrown a stone at it, let it escape and both shoot it as it ran. It wouldn't have escaped us.

'We'll do that another time,' said Philippe.

'I'm glad you pointed the hare out to me, Philippe, there aren't many hunters like you.'

'I wouldn't do it for everyone,' said Philippe.

The Lizard

I

Born spontaneously of the cracked stone against which I'm leaning, he creeps up onto my shoulder, imagining I'm an extension of the wall, because I don't move and because my coat's the same grey colour. Flattering, even so.

II

WALL: What's causing my back to quiver?
LIZARD: IT'S ME.

The Green Lizard

Mind the paint!

The Grass Snake

What belly did this turd fall from?

The Weasel

Poor but clean, distinguished, she hops her way across the road and back, and, moving from one ditch to another and from hole to hole, she gives her private lessons.

The Hedgehog

Wipe your... if you please

II

You must accept me as I am and not squeeze me too
hard.

The Snake

I

Too long.

II

One tenth of a millionth of a quarter of Earth's meridian.

The Worm

Here's one that stretches and lengthens like a lovely noodle.

The Frogs

They oil their springs with sudden thrusts.

They leap out of the grass like heavy drops of frying-oil.

They settle, bronze paper-weights, on the wide leaves of the water-lily.

One gorges himself with air. You could put a coin through his mouth into his belly's cashbox.

They emerge, like sighs, from the mud.

Motionless, they are like huge eyes at water level, tumours on the flat pond.

Squatting cross-legged, stupefied, they yawn at the setting sun.

Then, like hawkers filling the streets with their racket, they cry out the latest news.

They're giving a party this evening; can you hear them rinsing their glasses?

Occasionally they snap up an insect.

And some of them spend all their time making love.

And all of them tempt the fisherman.

Without difficulty, I break off a switch. I have a pin on my overcoat that I bend into a hook.

There's no lack of string.

But I still need a wisp of yarn, of something red.

I look through my pockets, search the ground, the sky.

I find nothing and, ready and waiting, stare sadly at my buttonhole which – this is no reproach – there has been no hurry to decorate with red ribbon.[1]

---

1 An oblique reference to the Légion d'Honneur.

The Toad

Born of a stone, he lives beneath a stone and will dig his grave there.

I visit him frequently, and each time I lift his stone I'm afraid of finding him and afraid he'll no longer be there.

He is.

Hidden in this refuge that is dry, clean, confined, all his own, he occupies it fully, bloated like a miser's purse.

If a downpour drives him out, he comes right up to me. After a few heavy jumps he rests on his haunches and looks at me with reddened eyes.

If an unjust world treats him like a leper, I'm not afraid of crouching close and lowering my human face to his.

I shall then overcome what's left of my revulsion and caress you, toad, with my hand!

Some things we swallow in life taste much worse.

Even so, yesterday I showed a lack of tact. He was fermenting and seeping from all his fissured warts.

'My poor friend,' I said to him, 'I don't wish to hurt your feelings, but my God you're ugly!'

He opened his childish toothless mouth with its warm breath, and replied with a faintly English accent:

'And you're not?'

The Grasshopper

Could he be the gendarme among insects?

All day long he leaps about in furious pursuit of invisible poachers he never catches.

The tallest grasses fail to stop him.

Nothing frightens him, for he has seven-league boots, a bull-neck, the brow of a genius, the belly of a ship's hull, celluloid wings, devil's horns and a huge sabre on his backside.

Since one cannot have the virtues of a gendarme without his vices, the grasshopper, it has to be admitted, chews tobacco.

If you think I'm lying, follow him with your fingers, play puss-in-the-corner with him, and when you catch him, between leaps, on a leaf of lucerne grass, observe his mouth: it secretes through his mandibles a black foam that looks like tobacco juice.

But you can't contain him any longer. His mania for leaping takes hold of him again. With a sudden effort the green monster escapes from your grasp and, fragile, easily dismantled, leaves a tiny thigh in your hand.

The Cricket

It is the hour when, weary of wandering, the black insect returns from his outing and carefully restores order to his estate.

First he rakes his narrow sandy paths.

He makes sawdust, which he scatters outside the door of his retreat.

He files the root of this tall blade likely to annoy him.

He rests.

Then he winds up his tiny watch.

Has he finished? Is it broken? He rests again for a while.

He goes inside and shuts the door.

For an age he turns his key in the delicate lock.

And he listens: nothing untoward outside.

But he does not feel safe.

And as if by a tiny chain on a creaking pulley, he lowers himself into the bowels of the earth.

Nothing more is heard.

In the silent countryside the poplars rise like fingers in the air, pointing to the moon.

The Cockroach

Black and flattened like a keyhole.

The Glow-Worm

I

What's going on? Nine o'clock at night and his
light's still on.

II

This drop of moon in the grass!

The Spider

I

A hairy little black fist, clutching strands of hair.

II

All night long, in the name of the moon, she affixes her seals.

The Cockchafer

I

A late bud opens and flies from the chestnut tree.

II

Heavier than air, scarcely able to steer, stubborn and grumbling, it nonetheless reaches its destination, with its chocolate wings.

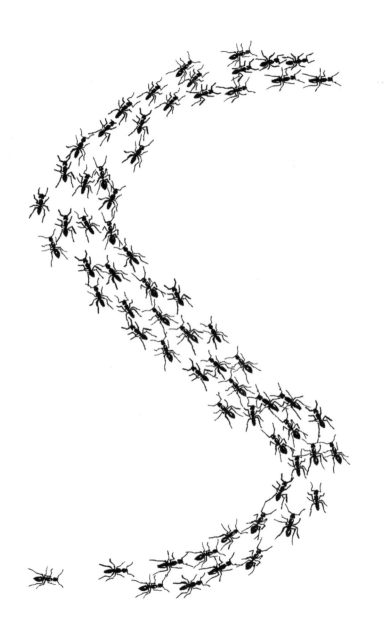

Ants

I

Each of them looks like the figure three.

And there are masses and masses of them!

There are 333333333333... to infinity.

II

The Ant and the Partridge

An ant falls into a rut full of rain water and is about to drown, when a partridge, who was drinking there, plucks it out with his beak and saves its life.

'I shall do the same for you,' says the ant.

'The days of La Fontaine,' replies the sceptical partridge, 'are long since past. Not that I doubt your gratitude, but how would you set about biting the heel of a hunter about to shoot me! Hunters today do not walk barefoot.'

The ant wastes no energy in arguing and hurries off to rejoin his sisters, all of whom were following the same path, like black beads being strung.

Now, the hunter was not far away.

He was resting on his side beneath a tree. He sees the partridge, running and pecking its way through the stubble. He gets to his feet and is about to fire, but his right arm had gone to sleep.[1] He cannot raise his gun. His arm drops inert to his side, and the partridge does not wait for it to lose its numbness.

---

1   An untranslatable pun on '*fourmi*' ('ant') and '*avoir des fourmis dans les jambes*' ('to have pins and needles in one's legs'). 'J'ai des fourmis dans le bras' means 'My arm has gone to sleep'.

The Snail

I

In the season of colds the snail stays at home, his giraffe-neck pulled in, boiling like a stuffed nose.

When fine weather comes he goes for a stroll, but can only walk on his tongue.

II

My little friend Abel was playing with his snails.

He's raising a whole boxful and, to tell them apart, he has numbered their shells with a pencil.

If the weather's too dry, the snails sleep in the box. As soon as rain threatens, Abel lines them up outside, and if the rain is slow to fall, he wakes them up by pouring a pot of water over them. And all of them, he says, except the mothers brooding in the bottom of the box, are guarded by a dog called Barbare – a strip of lead that Abel pushes along with his thumb.

When I talked to him about the difficulties of training snails, I noticed that he shook his head, even when he was saying yes.

'Abel,' I said, 'why does your head move like that from right to left?'

'It's my sugar,' Abel said.

'What sugar?'

'Here – look!'

While he was kneeling on all fours to prevent number 8 from getting away, I saw on Abel's neck, between his skin and his shirt, a lump of sugar hanging from a thread, like a medal.

'Mother ties it on me,' he said, 'when she wants to punish me.'

'Does that bother you?'

'It scratches.'

'And it stings too, huh? The skin's all red.'

'But when she forgives me,' Abel says, 'I eat it.'

The Caterpillar

He emerges from a tuft of grass that had hidden him during the heat. With huge undulations he crosses the sandy path. He is careful not to stop, and for a moment he thinks he is lost in the gardener's footprint.

Having reached the strawberries, he takes a rest, raises his nose and sniffs from right to left; then sets off again; and under the leaves and over the leaves he knows now where he's going.

What a beautiful caterpillar, fat, hairy, furry, brown with gold specks and those jet-black eyes!

Guided by his sense of smell, he quivers and puckers like a thick eyebrow.

He stops at the foot of a rose tree.

With his delicate pads he tests the rough bark, sways his little puppy head and decides to climb.

And this time, you'd think he was painfully swallowing each bit of the way.

At the very top of the tree a rose, with an innocent girl's complexion, was blooming. The rose intoxicates herself with the scent she sheds on the air. She mistrusts no one. The first caterpillar who so wishes may climb up her stem. She receives him like a gift.

And, anticipating a cold night, she's glad to put a fur boa round her neck.

The Flea

A speck of tobacco on springs.

The Butterfly

A billet-doux folded in half looking for a flower's address.

The Wasp

But she'll end up ruining her figure!

The Dragonfly

She's treating her pink-eye.

From one riverbank to the other, she keeps dipping her swollen eyes in the cool water.

And she crackles, as though flying by electricity.

The Squirrel

I

A plume! What panache! Well yes, my little friend, but that's not the place you're supposed to wear it.[1]

II

Nimble igniter of autumn, he moves the little torch of his tail this way and that beneath the leaves.

---

1 'Ralliez-vous à mon panache blanc!' was the rallying cry of Henri IV – and the 'panache' (plume feathers) was displayed on his helmet.

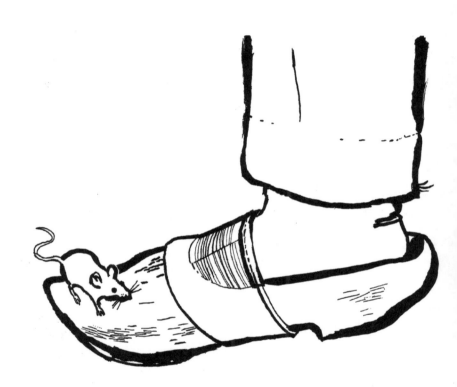

The Mouse

As I sit beneath the lamp, writing my daily page, I hear a faint noise. If I stop, it stops. It starts again as soon as my pen scratches the paper.

It's a mouse waking up.

I sense her scurrying around the dark corner where our maid keeps her dusters and brushes.

The mouse jumps to the floor and scampers across the kitchen tiles. She passes near the fireplace, under the sink, disappears among the dishes, and spying out the land further and further afield, she approaches me.

Each time I set down my pen, the silence alarms her. Each time I put pen to paper, she thinks perhaps that another mouse is somewhere near, and feels reassured.

Then I lose sight of her. She's under my table, between my feet. She moves from one chair leg to the next. She brushes against my clogs, nibbles the wood, or, boldly climbs onto them!

I mustn't move my leg or breathe too deeply – otherwise, she'd scamper off.

But I must continue to write and, for fear she might abandon me to my solitude, I scribble signs, I doodle, no matter what, daintily, the way she nibbles.

Monkeys

Go and look at the monkeys (naughty boys, they've torn the seat of their pants!) climb, dance in the new sun, lose their temper, scratch themselves, peel things, and drink with a primitive grace, while their eyes, dulled at times, flash with sparks that are quickly extinguished.

Go and look at the flamingos who walk on tongs for fear of wetting their pink petticoats in the pond; the swans and the vainglorious plumbing[1] of their necks; the ostrich with his baby chicken wings and his dutiful stationmaster's cap; the storks who are constantly shrugging their shoulders (which is meaningless after a while); the marabou shivering in its wretched little jacket; the penguins in their Inverness capes; the pelican brandishing his beak like a wooden sabre; and the parakeets, the tamest of which are less tame than their keeper, who ends up taking a ten-sou coin from my hand.

Go and look at the yak, laden with prehistoric thoughts; the giraffe who shows us, above the bars of her cage, her head on the end of a pike; the elephant who, stooping and nose to the ground, scuffs his slippers in front of his door: he almost disappears in the sack of his trousers that are pulled up too high and from which, behind, a little piece of rope dangles.

Do go and look at the porcupine covered with quills that are most inconvenient for him and his lady-friend; the zebra, a black-lined model for all other zebras; the panther who's now reduced to a bed-side rug;[2] the bear who amuses us but scarcely himself; and the lion who yawns and makes us yawn.

---

1 A reference to the contemporary design of taps which sometimes took the shape of a swan's neck.

2 '*La panthère descendue au pied de son lit*'. Untranslatable pun: 'descendre' means descend; 'une descente' means a bed-side rug.

The Stag

I entered the wood at one end of the path, as he was coming in at the other.

I thought at first that a stranger was approaching with a plant on his head.

Then I observed the little dwarf tree, with its bare spreading branches.

Finally the stag came into full view and we both stopped.

I told him:

'Come closer. There's nothing to fear. If I'm carrying a rifle, it's only to appear bold, to look like a man who takes himself seriously. I never use it and I leave the cartridges in a drawer.'

The stag listened and sniffed suspiciously at my words. As soon as I stopped talking, he lost no time: his legs moved like stalks being crossed and uncrossed by the wind. He fled.

'What a pity!' I cried. 'I was already dreaming of us walking along together – I feeding you by hand your favourite grasses, you at a leisurely pace carrying my rifle across your antlers.'

The Gudgeon

I

He swims upstream and follows the path the pebbles make: because he doesn't care for mud or weeds.

He catches sight of a bottle lying on a bed of sand. It contains nothing but water. I forgot on purpose to put any bait inside. The gudgeon swims round it, looks for the entrance – and now he's caught.

I pull in the bottle and throw back the gudgeon.

Further upstream, he hears a noise. Rather than flee, he draws near, out of curiosity. It's me having fun, wading in the water, stirring up the bottom with a stick, with a net alongside. The gudgeon stubbornly tries to swim through the mesh. He gets stuck.

I pull up the net and throw back the gudgeon.

Downstream, a sudden jerk tightens my line, and the bi-coloured float dips beneath the surface.

I tug at the line and it's him again.

I unhook him and throw him back.

I won't catch him next time.

There he is, motionless below me, in the clear water. I can make out his broad head, his big, stupid eye and his barbels.

He yawns with his torn lip, panting hard after such a commotion.

But he's incorrigible.
I drop my line again, with the same worm.
And instantly, the gudgeon bites.
Which of us will be the first to tire?

II

They've definitely decided not to bite. Don't they know the fishing season opened today!

The Pike

Motionless in the shade of a willow, he's the dagger concealed in the old bandit's cloak.

The Whale

She has enough whalebone in her mouth to make herself
a corset – but with a waist like that!…

Fish

Monsieur Vernet, as a fisherman, was neither pretentious, skilled, garrulous or unbearable; he had no special clothes, no expensive and useless tackle; and as the opening of the fishing season approached he felt no feverish excitement.

A single rod with a braided line sufficed him, a discreetly painted float, worms from his garden as bait, and a canvas bag in which he brought back the fish. Yet Monsieur Vernet liked fishing, not passionately, that would be to exaggerate; he liked it very much, it was all that he liked, having given up one after the other, for various reasons, his favourite forms of exercise.

Once the fishing season had opened, he fished almost every day, morning or evening, almost always at the same spot. Other fishermen attach importance to the wind, to the sun that warms, to the colour of the water. Monsieur Vernet did not. With his hazel fishing rod in hand, he would set out of his own sweet will, walk along the banks of the Yonne, stop as soon as he wished to go no further, let out his line, set down his rod, and spend many agreeable hours until it was time to return home for lunch or supper. Monsieur Vernet was not sufficiently eccentric to use fishing as an excuse to eat uncomfortably out of doors.

And so it was that he found himself, last Sunday morning, at an early hour, having made haste on this opening day, seated on the grass, and not on a folding seat, on the banks of the river.

At once he set about enjoying himself as much as he could. To him the morning seemed delicious, not only because he was fishing, but because he was breathing in the gentle air, because he was looking at the shimmering Yonne, following the path of long-legged mosquitoes on the water, and listening to the crickets behind him.

And it was true, the fishing also interested him, a great deal.

Soon he caught a fish.

This was no extraordinary event for Monsieur Vernet. He had caught others! He was not desperate to catch fish, he could do without them, but every time a fish bit too hard, it had to be tugged out of the water. And Monsieur Vernet always tugged with a little emotion. You could tell by the trembling of his fingers when they changed the bait.

Monsieur Vernet, before opening his bag, laid the gudgeon in the grass. It would be wrong to say: 'What! Is that all? A mere gudgeon?' There are big gudgeons which shake the rod so violently that a fisherman's heart beats as though this were real drama.

Monsieur Vernet, now calm, cast once more and, instead of putting the gudgeon in the bag, without knowing why (he could never explain), he looked at the gudgeon.

This was the first time he had ever looked at a fish he had just caught! Usually, he was in a hurry to cast again to catch other fish – fish that were waiting just for that. Today, he looked at the gudgeon with curiosity, then with astonishment, then with a sort of disquiet.

The gudgeon, after several convulsions which quickly sapped its strength, came to rest on its side and gave no further sign of life, except for the visible efforts it made to breathe.

Fins glued to its back, it opened and closed its mouth, whose bottom lip was adorned with two barbels, like soft little moustaches.

And, slowly, breathing became more painful, until finally the jaws could not quite close.

'Funny,' Monsieur Vernet said, 'I can see that it's suffocating!'

And he added:

'How it suffers!'

This was a new observation, as clear as it was unexpected. Yes, fish suffer when they die; you are unaware of it at first, because they don't tell you. They express nothing; they are mute, there's no doubt about it; and in its death-throes, this gudgeon still seemed to be playing!

To see fish die, you must watch them carefully, by chance, like Monsieur Vernet. It doesn't matter as long as you don't think about it, but as soon as you do!...

'I know myself,' Monsieur Vernet told himself, 'I'm done for; I question myself, and feel I must now complete the questionnaire; it's no use resisting the temptation to be logical: fear of ridicule will not stop me; first hunting, now fishing! One day, while hunting, I asked myself after one of my crimes: what right have you to do that? I was ready with the reply. One quickly observes how repugnant it is to break the wing of a partridge, the legs of a hare. In the evening I hung up my gun that will never kill again. The odiousness of fishing, which is less bloody, has only just struck me.'

As he spoke, M. Vernet saw his float dance on the water, as though in defiance. He tugged at his line, mechanically, one more time. It was a perch, spiky and prickly, which, gluttonous like all of its kind, had swallowed the hook right down into its belly. M. Vernet had to retrieve it, rip it from the flesh, tear red-silk gills, make his hands sticky with blood.

Ah! How the fish was bleeding, how it expressed itself!

Monsieur Vernet reeled in his line, hid the two fish at the foot of a willow, hoping that an otter would find them, and left.

He seemed in rather merry mood and meditated as he walked.

'There is no excuse,' he was telling himself. 'As a hunter, even when I bought other types of meat with my money, I at least used to eat the game, I fed myself, I did not kill just for pleasure – but Madame Vernet laughs when I bring her my wretched few fish that are stiff and dry, and I am ashamed to ask her to cook them. It's the cat who has a feast. Let him catch the fish himself, if he so wishes. I shall destroy my rod!'

Yet as he still held the broken rod in his hands, Monsieur Vernet murmured, not without sadness:

Am I growing wise at last, or am I losing the taste for life?

In the Garden

THE SPADE: *Fac et spera.*[1]
THE PICK: That's what I say too.

THE FLOWERS: Will it be sunny today?
THE SUNFLOWER: Yes, if I wish it.
THE WATERING-CAN: Excuse me, but if I want, it will rain, and, if I remove my nozzle, in torrents.

THE ROSEBUSH: Ah! What a wind!
THE STAKE: I'm here.

THE RASPBERRY: Why do roses have thorns? You can't eat a rose.
THE CARP IN THE POND: Well said! It's because they eat me that I prick them with my spines.
THE THISTLE: Yes, but too late.

THE ROSE: Do you think I'm beautiful?
THE HORNET: I'd have to look at your petticoat.
THE ROSE: Enter.

THE BEE: Keep it up! Everyone says I'm a good worker. I hope by the end of the month to be promoted to department head.

117

THE VIOLETS: We have all had honours conferred on us.

THE WHITE VIOLETS: All the more reason to be modest, my sisters.

THE LEEK: Exactly. Am I bragging?

THE SPINACH: It's me who's the sorrel.

THE SORREL: No no, it's me.

THE SHALLOT: Ugh! What an awful smell.

THE GARLIC: I bet it's that carnation again.

THE ASPARAGUS: My little finger tells me all.

THE POTATO: I think I've just had babies.

APPLE TREE TO THE PEAR TREE OPPOSITE: It's your pear, your pear, your pear… it's your pear I'd like to grow.

---

1 The motto printed on the cover of books published by Alphonse Lemerre, above an illustration of a little naked man digging the soil with his spade.

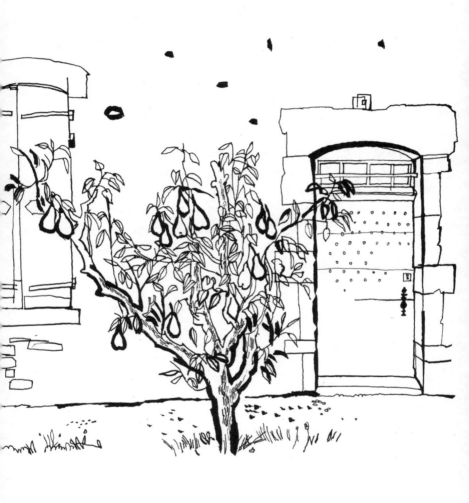

The Poppies

They explode in the cornfield like an army of little soldiers; but though their red's far more exquisite, they are harmless.

Their sword is a blade of wheat.

It's the wind that makes them run, and any poppy may linger, when he wants to, at the edge of a furrow, with the cornflower, its compatriot.

The Vineyard

All its vines, props upright, are shouldering arms.

What are they waiting for? There will be no more grapes this year, and vine leaves are now only used on statues.

Bats

Night's getting worn out with use.

Not worn out up above, where the stars are. It's worn out like a dress trailing along the ground, among stones and trees, right down to the depths of unwholesome tunnels and damp caves.

Shards of night penetrate every nook and cranny. Thorns puncture it, frosts crack it, mud besmirches it. And every morning, when night recedes, a few tatters break loose and get caught here and there.

That's how bats are born.

And it's due to their origin that they cannot stand the light of day.

After the sun has set, when we are taking the air, they detach themselves from the old rafters, where they were hanging lethargically by one talon.

Their awkward flight disturbs us. On featherless, whaleboned wings they flutter around us. They find their way by ear, not with their useless, defective eyes.

My friend hides her face, and I turn my head away, fearing their foul touch.

It is said that even more passionately than we make love, they would suck our blood until we died.

How people exaggerate!

They mean no harm. They never touch us.

Daughters of night, all they hate is light, and, rustling their miniscule funereal shawls, they search for candles to extinguish.

The Cage without Birds

Felix does not understand how people can imprison birds in cages.

'And it's also a crime,' he says, 'to pick flowers, and, personally, I'd rather smell them on their stems – just as birds are meant to fly.

Yet he buys a cage; he hangs it in his window. He puts a nest of cotton-wool inside, a saucer of grain, a cup of fresh and renewable water. He also hangs a swing there and a little mirror.

And if, surprised, you question him:

'I congratulate myself on my generosity,' he says, 'each time I look at this cage. I could put a bird in there, and I leave it empty. A brown thrush, if I wished, a smart bullfinch who loves to hop, or any of our many birds could be captured. Thanks to me, at least one of them stays free. That's at least something.'

The Canary

What on earth made me buy that bird?

The bird-seller told me: 'It's a male. Give him a week to get used to his new surroundings, and he will sing.'

The bird, however, remains obstinately silent and does everything wrong.

As soon as I fill his cup with grain, he attacks it with his beak and scatters it to the four winds.

I tie a biscuit between two bars with a piece of string. The string is all he eats. He pushes away the biscuit and hits it as though with a hammer, and the biscuit falls.

He bathes in his clean water and drinks the water from his bathtub. He shits in both, at random.

He imagines that canary bread is made expressly for birds of his kind to nest in, and instinctively he snuggles down there.

He hasn't yet learnt what lettuce leaves are for, and merely delights in tearing them to pieces.

When he picks up a seed with the serious intent of swallowing it, it's painful to behold. He rolls it from one corner of the cage to another with his beak, squeezes and crushes it, and twists his head, like a little old man with no teeth.

His sugar lump is never of any use to him. Is it a jutting stone, a balcony, or a not very practical table?

He prefers instead his little sticks of wood. There are two that cross, one above the other, and it makes me sick to watch him hop to and fro. He reminds me of the mechanical stupidity of a pendulum on a clock that does not tell the time. What pleasure does he get from hopping like that? Out of what necessity does he do it?

If he takes a rest from all this dreary gymnastics, and balances with one foot on the perch which he strangles with his claws, his other foot mechanically searches for the same perch.

As soon as winter arrives, and the stove is lit, he thinks that spring is here, that the time has come to moult, and he sheds his feathers.

The glow from my lamp disturbs his nights, disrupts his sleeping pattern. He goes to bed at dusk. I let darkness settle around him. Perhaps he dreams? Suddenly, I approach his cage with the lamp. He opens his eyes. What? Daylight already? And he quickly starts to move about, dance, peck at a leaf, fan his tail, stretch his wings.

But I blow out the lamp and regret I can't see his bewildered face.

I've soon had enough of this silent bird who lives all back-to-front, and I put him out of the window … He has no more idea of what do with freedom than how to use a cage. He will have to be picked up by hand.

But don't try bringing him back to me!

Not only shall I offer no reward, I shall swear I don't know the bird.

The Finch

At the edge of the barn roof, a finch is singing. He repeats, at irregular intervals, his hereditary note. By dint of looking, the eye blurs and can no longer distinguish him from the massive barn. The entire life of these stones, this hay, these beams and these tiles vanishes because of a bird's song.

Or rather, the barn itself whistles a little tune.

The Nest of Goldfinches

There was a pretty nest of goldfinches in the forked branch of our cherry tree – round, perfect, all horsehair outside, all down inside, and four nestlings had just hatched. I said to my father:

'I'm tempted to take them and raise them myself.'

My father had often explained to me that it was a crime to put birds in a cage. But this time, tired no doubt of repeating the same thing, he found nothing to say. A few days later I said to him:

'If I decide to do it, it will be easy. First I'll put the nest in a cage, then I'll fasten the cage to the tree, and the mother will feed the little ones through the bars until they no longer need her.'

My father did not tell me what he thought of this scheme.

Which is why I put the nest in a cage, the cage in the cherry tree, and what I had anticipated now occurred: the adult goldfinches, with no hesitation, brought beakfuls of caterpillars to their young. And my father, as amused as I was, observed from a distance their colourful comings and goings, their blood-red and sulphur-yellow flight.

One evening I said:

'The little ones are now full-fledged. If they were free, they'd fly away. Let them spend one final night together as a family, and tomorrow I'll take them into the house and hang the cage in my window, and believe you me – there'll be no goldfinches in the world better cared for.'

My father did not argue.

The next day I found the cage empty. My father stood there, witnessing my amazement.

'I'm not asking,' I said, 'but I'd love to know what idiot opened that cage door!'

The Oriole

I tell him:

    'Give me back that cherry, at once.'

    'Fine,' replies the oriole.

    He gives back the cherry, and with the cherry the three hundred thousand noxious larvae he swallows in a year.

The Sparrow

Seated beneath the hazels in our garden, I listen to the sounds that every trusting tree makes through its leaves, its insects and its birds.

Silent, inanimate as we approach, it begins to live once more as soon as it believes we have gone, because we, like it, keep silent.

After the visit of a goldfinch, who flies about in the hazels, pecks a little at the leaves and flies away without noticing me, a sparrow alights on a branch above my head.

Although full-fledged, she must have been young. She grips the branch with her claws, she does not stir, as if tired from flying, and she cheeps with her tender bill. She cannot see me and I gaze at her for a long time. Then I need to move. As I stir, the sparrow opens her wings a little and closes them again without alarm.

I don't know why, but I stand up, involuntarily, and with my hand held out, I call her quietly.

The sparrow flies down awkwardly from her branch onto my finger!

I feel moved, like a man who suddenly wakens to a spell, like a dreamer who smiled by mistake at an unknown woman and sees her return the smile.

The trusting sparrow flutters its wings to keep her balance on the tip of my finger, and its bill is ready to swallow anything.

As I set off to show the sparrow to my family who will surely be amazed, Raoul, our little neighbour, who seems to be looking for something, comes running up:

'Ah! You've found her?' he said.

'Yes, young man, I know how to catch birds!'

'She escaped from her cage,' said Raoul, 'I've been looking for her all morning.'

'Is she yours, then?'

'Yes, sir. I've been raising her for a week. She's started to make long flights, and she's still very tame.'

'Take your sparrow, Raoul; but if you let her escape again, I'll strangle her – she frightens me!'

Swallows

I

They give me my daily lesson.

They stipple the air with little cries.

They draw a straight line, place a comma at the end, and, suddenly, start a new paragraph.

They put the house where I live between wild parentheses.

Too swift for the garden pond to make a copy of their flight, they soar from cellar to garret.

With their light feather quills, they inscribe matchless signatures.

Then, in pairs, entwined, they mingle and spatter ink against the blue of the sky.

But only the eye of a friend can follow them; you may know Latin and Greek, but I can read the unknown language these chimney swallows trace on the air.

II

THE FINCH: If you ask me, swallows are stupid: they think a chimney's a tree.

THE BAT: You can say what you like, but compared with me they fly badly: in broad daylight, they always go in the wrong direction; if they flew at night, like I do, they would kill themselves every second.

III

A dozen white-rumped swallows below me intersect one another in flight with a restless and silent ardour, as though in the narrow confines of an aviary. Like seamstresses before my very nose weaving hurriedly against time.

What are they looking for, bewildered, in the air riddled with their flight. Are they seeking shelter? Are they saying farewell to me? Motionless, I feel the freshness of their light breath, and I fear, I hope that two of these demented creatures will collide. But with a skill that dashes my hopes, they suddenly vanish without collision.

The Magpie

I

There's always a patch of last winter's snow on him.

Feet together, he hops along the ground, then, flying mechanically and straight, makes for a tree.

Sometimes he misses and can only stop on the next one.

Commonplace, so despised that he seems immortal, wearing evening attire in the morning so he can chatter till nightfall, insufferable in his tails, he is the most truly French of our birds.

II

THE MAGPIE: Cacacacacaca.

THE FROG: What's he saying?

THE MAGPIE: I'm not saying, I'm singing.

THE FROG: Croak!

THE MOLE: Quiet up there, we can't hear ourselves work!

Blackbird!

In my garden there's an old, almost dead walnut tree which frightens the little birds. A single black bird lives among the few remaining leaves.

But the rest of the garden is full of young, flowering trees where cheerful, lively birds of all colours nest.

And it seems that these young trees mock the old walnut tree. They continually hurl flocks of chattering birds at it, as though teasing it with a flurry of words.

Sparrows, martins, tits and finches torment it in turn. With their wings they strike the tip of its branches. The air crackles with their tiny cries; then they make off, and another pestering gang sets out from the young trees, flouting, squealing, whistling and warbling with all its might.

Thus, from dawn to dusk, like mocking words, finches, tits, starlings and sparrows break out from the young trees and make for the old walnut tree.

But sometimes the walnut tree grows impatient, it stirs its remaining leaves, releases its black bird and replies:

Merle.[1]

---

1 Untranslatable: '*merle*' means blackbird; '*merde*' means shit.

II

THE JAY: Always in black, you nasty blackbird!

THE BLACKBIRD: If you please, Mr Deputy Prefect, that's all I have to wear.

The Parrot

Not so bad! And there was some point in him, when animals did not speak, but nowadays all animals have talent.

The Lark

I

I've never seen a lark and it's no use getting up with the dawn. The lark is not a bird of the earth.

Since early morning I've been tramping over clods of earth and dry grass.

Flocks of grey sparrows and brightly painted goldfinches hover over the thorn hedges.

The jay, in official uniform, inspects the trees.

A quail skims the lucerne and traces with chalk the line of its flight.

Behind the shepherd, who knits better than any woman, the sheep follow, looking all the same.

And all is steeped in a light so new that even the crow, who bodes no good, makes you smile.

But listen the way I listen.

Can you hear, somewhere up there, pieces of crystal being crushed in a golden bowl?

Who can tell where the lark is singing?

If I look up into the air, the sun burns my eyes.

I have to give up trying to see it.

The lark lives in the sky, and it's the only bird of the sky whose song can reach us.

II

She falls to the ground, dead drunk from having once again poked the sun's eye.

The Kingfisher

Not a bite, this evening, but I had a rare experience.

As I was holding out my fishing rod, a kingfisher came and perched on it.

There is no bird more brilliant.

He was like a great blue flower at the tip of a long stem. The rod bent beneath the weight. I held my breath, so proud to be taken for a tree by a kingfisher.

And I'm sure he did not fly off from fear, but thought he was simply flitting from one branch to another.

The Sparrow-Hawk

He begins by describing circles over the village.

He was a mere fly, a speck of soot.

He grows larger as the circles shrink.

Sometimes he remains motionless. The poultry show signs of alarm. The pigeons return to the rooftop. A hen, with a sharp cry, calls back her chicks, and the watchful geese can be heard cackling from barnyard to barnyard.

The sparrow-hawk hesitates and hovers at the same height. Perhaps all he objects to is the weathercock on the steeple.

He seems suspended in the sky by a thread.

Suddenly the thread snaps, the sparrow-hawk swoops, his victim chosen. This is the moment of drama, here below.

But to everyone's amazement, he stops before reaching the ground, as though he lacked weight, and with a flap of his wings he once more climbs the sky.

He's seen me lying in wait for him at my door, holding behind my back something long that gleams.

The Wagtail

She runs as much as she flies, and always under our feet
– familiar, uncatchable, she dares us, with her little cries,
to step on her tail.

The Jay

The Deputy Prefect of the fields.

The Crow

I

The grave accent on the furrow.

II

'*Wha? Wha? Wha?*'
'Nothing.'

III

The crows fly beneath a blue and seamless sky. Suddenly, one of them, at the very front, slows down and draws a large circle. The others turn behind him. Bored with the journey, they seem to be dancing a round and preening themselves, with their wings stretched, like the pleats of a skirt.

          …A crow

   Just now foretold misfortune for some bird.
   I seized my gun and killed the crow.
   He was not mistaken.[1]

---

1 La Fontaine, *Les deux pigeons*.

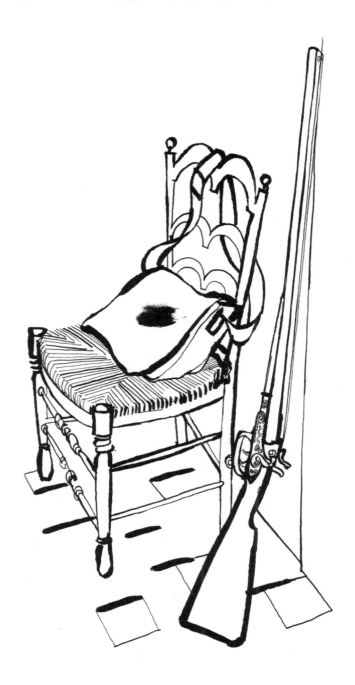

The Partridges

The partridge and the ploughman live in peace, he behind his plough, she in the neighbouring lucerne, the right distance apart for neither of them to get in each other's way. The partridge knows the ploughman's voice, she is not afraid when he shouts or swears.

If the plough creaks or the ox coughs or the donkey brays, she knows it's nothing.

And this peace lasts until I disturb it.

When I arrive, the partridge flies off, the ploughman is ill at ease, and so are the ox and the donkey. I fire, and the commotion caused by an intruder throws all nature into confusion.

First of all, I flush these partridges from the stubble, then from the lucerne, then from a meadow, then from all along a hedge, then from the top of a wood, then...

And all of a sudden I stop, in a sweat, and exclaim:

'Those damned birds are making me run!'

From a distance, I noticed something at the foot of a tree, in the middle of the meadow.

I draw near the hedge and peer over it.

It seems that a bird's neck is sticking out from the shadow of a tree. Immediately my heart beats faster. There can only be partridges in that grass. As soon as she heard me, the mother, by a signal they all know, told them to lie low. She herself has huddled down. Only her head remains upright, as she keeps watch. But I hesitate, because the head does not move, and I'm afraid of making a mistake, of firing at a root.

Here and there, around the tree, yellow patches – partridges or lumps of earth – further disturb my vision.

If I flush the birds, the branches of the tree will prevent me from firing at them in flight, and I prefer, by shooting at them on the ground, to commit what serious hunters call a murder.

But what I take to be the head of a partridge still does not move.

For a long time I lie low and watch.

If it really is a partridge, her immobility and vigilance are remarkable, and all the others, in the manner they obey her, deserve this guardian. Not one moves.

I make a feint. I hide my whole body behind the hedge and stop watching, for as long as I can see the partridge, she can see me.

Now we are all invisible, amid a deathly silence.

Then I look again.

Ah! This time I'm certain! The partridge thinks I have disappeared. The neck has risen, and the movement she makes to pull it in gives her away.

Slowly I lift the butt of my rifle to my shoulder…

In the evening, weary and sated, before falling into a game-filled sleep, I think of the partridges I hunted throughout the day, and I imagine the night they are spending.

They are panic-stricken.

Why do some not come when called?

Why are some in pain and, pecking at their wounds, unable to keep still?

And why are they now all so terrified?

No sooner do they settle, than the sentinel sounds the alarm. They must set off again, leave the grass or the stubble.

They do nothing but flee, and are frightened even by familiar noises.

They no longer frolic, they no longer eat, they no longer sleep.

They are at a loss to understand what's going on.

If the feather that falls from a wounded partridge were to tuck itself into my proud huntsman's hat, I wouldn't find that at all extraordinary.

As soon as it rains too much, or it's too dry, or my dog loses the scent, or I aim badly and the partridges become unapproachable, I regard myself to be in a state of legitimate defence.

There are birds – magpies, jays, blackbirds, thrushes – which no self-respecting hunter will fight, and I respect myself.

I only enjoy fighting partridges!

They are so cunning!

One of their tricks is to fly ahead of you, but you catch up with them and teach them a lesson.

Another is to wait until the hunter has passed, but they fly up too soon behind his back, and he whirls round.

Another is to hide in deep lucerne, but he makes straight for it.

Another is to turn sharply in flight, but in so doing they come closer together.

Another is to run instead of fly, and they run faster than a man, but there's the dog.

Another is to call to each other when they scatter, but in doing so they also call the hunter, and there is nothing he likes more than a partridge's song.

This young pair had already started living by themselves. I surprised them one evening at the edge of a ploughed field. They flew up so closely entwined, wings almost linked, that the shot which killed one shattered the other.

The one saw nothing and felt nothing, but the other had time to see his mate dead and feel himself die beside her.

They both left behind, on the same bit of earth, a little love, a little blood and a few feathers.

Hunter, with a single shot you killed two splendid birds – go and tell your family all about it.

These two old partridges from last year, whose brood had been destroyed, loved each other no less than the young ones. I always saw them together. They were very clever at avoiding me and I did not pursue them relentlessly. It was by chance that I killed one. And then I looked for the other, to kill it as well, out of pity!

This one has a broken leg, hanging down, as if I were holding it by a thread.

That one follows the others until his wings fail him; it collapses and runs – runs as fast as it can in front of the dog, lightly and half out of the furrow.

This one received a lead pellet in its head. It separates itself from the others. Stunned, it rises into the air, climbs higher than the trees, higher than the vane on the steeple, towards the sun. And the hunter, filled with anxiety, loses sight of it, when finally it yields to the weight of its heavy head. It closes its wings, and plummets, beak first, like an arrow into the ground.

That one falls without a sound, like a rag flung at a dog's nose to train it.

Another, when the gun goes off, wavers like a little boat and capsizes.

You have no idea why this one died, so hidden is the wound beneath the feathers.

I quickly stuff this one into my pocket, as though afraid of being seen, of seeing myself.

But I have to strangle the one that does not want to die. Between my fingers she claws the air, opens her beak, her delicate tongue flutters, and the shadow of death, as Homer says, descends on her eyes.

Over there, the peasant lifts his head at my shot and stares at me.

That labourer is going to pass judgment; he's going to speak to me; with his solemn voice he will put me to shame.

But no: sometimes it's an envious peasant, sulking because he can't go hunting like me, and sometimes it's a good-natured honest fellow whom I amuse and who tells me where my partridges have gone.

It's never the indignant spokesman of nature herself.

I reach home this morning, after five hours of walking, with my game-bag empty, my head lowered, my rifle heavy. The heat suggests an impending storm, and my exhausted dog walks slowly ahead of me with small steps, follows the hedges and often sits down in the shade of a tree and waits for me to catch up.

Suddenly, as I cross a field of lucerne, he falls or rather lies flat on the ground and waits, resolutely, motionless as a vegetable. Only the hairs at the tip of his tail quiver. I bet there are partridges under his nose. They are there, squeezed together, sheltering from the wind and the sun. They see the dog, they see me, perhaps they recognize me, and, terrified, they don't stir.

Wakened from my torpor, I am ready and wait.

My dog and I will not be the first to move.

Suddenly and simultaneously, the partridges rise up, still glued together as one, and my shot tears into them like a blow from my fist. One of them, stunned, does a pirouette. The dog leaps on it and brings me back a bloody rag, half a partridge. The fist did for the rest.

There! We are not returning empty-handed. The dog frolics and I swagger with pride.

What I deserve is a load of lead up my backside!

The Woodcock

I

All that was left of the April sun were a few pink-flecked clouds that no longer moved, as if they had arrived.

Night climbed from the earth and gradually clothed us in the narrow clearing, where my father lay in wait for the woodcock.

Standing next to him, the only thing I could clearly make out was its face. Taller than me, it could hardly see me, and the invisible dog breathed at our feet.

The thrushes were hurrying back to the wood, where the blackbird uttered its guttural cry, a sort of whinnying – an order for all the birds to be silent and sleep.

The woodcock was about to emerge from its retreat of dead leaves, and take to the air. When the weather is mild, as tonight, it lingers before reaching the plain. It circles above the woods and looks for a mate. By listening to its faint call, you can tell whether it's approaching or moving off. It flies heavily between the large oaks and its long beak hangs so low that it seems to be moving through the air with a little walking-stick.

As I was listening and looking in all directions, my father suddenly fired, but he didn't follow the dog who rushed off.

'Did you miss it?' I asked.

'I didn't shoot', he said. 'The gun went off in my hands.'

'All by itself?'

'Yes.'

'Ah!... A branch perhaps?'

'I don't know.'

I heard him pick up the empty cartridge.

'How were you holding it?'

Had he not understood?

'I'm asking you which way the gun was pointing?'

As he no longer replied, I didn't dare speak. Finally, I said to him:

'You could have killed... the dog '

'Let's go,' my father said.

II

The evening was mild, following a light drizzle. We leave at about five o'clock, we reach the wood and walk on leaves until sunset.

In the coppice, the dog covers more and more dog-miles. Can he smell the woodcock?

It matters little to the hunter, if he's a poet.

The hour had arrived when the woodcock utters its mating call, we take up our positions, too early, at the foot of a tree, at the edge of a clearing. The swift flight of the thrushes and blackbirds grazes the heart. The barrel of the gun stirs with impatience. Excitement at every noise! The ears tingle and the eye clouds over, and the moment passes so quickly... that it's already too late.

The woodcocks will not fly up again this evening.

You can't sleep there, poet!

Go home; because it's night, take the short cut across the damp meadows, where your shoes will flatten the soft little huts of the moles; return to the warmth, the light, without remorse, since you are without woodcock – unless you left yours at home![1]

---

1 Untranslatable pun: '*bécasse*' means 'woodcock'/'old woman'.

A Family of Trees

It was having crossed a sun-baked field that I encountered them.

They don't dwell by the side of the road, because of the noise. They inhabit uncultivated ground, near a spring known only to birds.

From afar, they seem impenetrable. As soon as I approach, their trunks separate. They greet me with caution. I can rest, refresh myself, but I sense they're watching me, distrustfully.

They live together as a family, the oldest in the middle, and the little ones, the ones whose first leaves have just been born, just about everywhere, but never too far away.

They take a long time to die, and their dead are left standing till they crumble to dust.

They stroke each other with their long branches, to make sure they are all there, like blind people. They gesticulate angrily if the wind wears itself out attempting to uproot them. But among themselves they never quarrel. They murmur only in agreement.

I feel they should be my real family. I shall quickly forget the other one. Little by little, these trees will adopt me, and to deserve it, I'm learning what I must know:

I know already how to watch the scudding clouds.

I know also how to stay in one place.

And I almost know how to be silent.

End of the Hunting Season

It's a poor day, grey and short, as though gnawed at both ends.

Towards noon, a sulky sun tries to pierce the mist, half-opens a pallid eye and immediately shuts it again.

I walk without direction. My gun is of no use to me, and my dog, usually so crazy, stays close by my side.

The water of the river is so limpid that it hurts: if you dipped your fingers in, it would cut them like broken glass.

In the stubble, wherever I tread, a listless lark whirrs up. They gather, whirl, and their flight scarcely disturbs the frozen air.

Over there, congregations of crows dig up the seeds of autumn.

Three partridges stand up in the middle of a field whose cropped grass no longer gives them cover.

How they've grown! They're young ladies now! They listen, anxiously. I've spotted them all right, but I leave them in peace and go on my way. And somewhere, no doubt, a trembling hare feels reassured and sets down his nose again on the edge of his lair.

All along this hedge (here and there a last leaf flutters its wings like a bird with a trapped leg), a blackbird flees at my approach, hides a little further off, then comes out under the dog's nose and, running no risk, makes fun of us.

Gradually, the mist thickens. It's as though I'm lost. My gun is no more than a stick in my hands that might go off. Where does this vague sound come from, this bleating, this tolling bell, this human cry?

I must get back. By a worn-down path, I return to the village. It alone knows its name. Humble peasants live there, and I'm the only one to visit them.

New Moon

The moon's nail is growing again.

The sun has disappeared. We turn round: the moon is there – she was following, wordlessly, modestly, in patient imitation.

The punctual moon has returned. The man with the aching heart was waiting in the darkness, so happy to see the moon that he no longer knows what he wanted to say to it.

Large white clouds draw near the full moon, like bears approaching a honeycomb.

The dreamer wears himself out watching the moon that has no hour or minute hand, indicating nothing, always nothing.

Suddenly, one feels ill at ease. It's the moon that now withdraws, carrying away our secrets. On the horizon, you can still just see it listening.

RICHARD STOKES is Visiting Professor of Lieder at the Royal Academy of Music. His previous translations include: *The Book of Lieder* (Faber), *A French Song Companion* (with Graham Johnson) (Faber), *The Spanish Song Companion* (with Jacqueline Cockburn) (Scarecrow Books), J.S. Bach: *The Complete Cantatas* (Scarecrow Books), Franz Kafka: *Metamorphosis* (Hesperus Press), Franz Kafka: *The Trial* (Hesperus Press), Franz Kafka: *Dearest Father* (with Hannah Stokes) (Oneworld Classics) and Alfred Brendel: *Playing the Human Game* (Phaidon Press).

LUCINDA ROGERS is best known for her reportage drawings of cities and urban life. She has produced illustrations for a wide variety of publications and clients including *The Guardian*, *The Independent*, *The Times*, *The New Yorker* and the Victoria and Albert Museum. She illustrated *The Dictionary of Urbanism* (Streetwise Press) and Rowley Leigh's *No Place Like Home* (Fourth Estate).